JUEL ANDERSEN'S
TEMPEH PRIMER

BOOKS BY JUEL ANDERSEN:

THE TOFU COOKBOOK (WITH CATHY BAUER)

JUEL ANDERSEN'S TOFU KITCHEN

TOFU PRIMER

TOFU FANTASIES

BY JUEL ANDERSEN & ROBIN CLUTE

CAROB PRIMER

JUEL ANDERSEN'S

TEMPEH PRIMER

A BEGINNER'S BOOK OF TEMPEH COOKERY

ROBIN CLUTE
JUEL ANDERSEN
WITH SIGRID ANDERSEN

Illustrations from: *Baby Days* Selections from Very Little Folks, Scribner & Co., N.Y. 1877. *Baby World* Selections from St. Nicholas, Century Co., N.Y. 1884

Illustrations by permission of Dover Publications, Inc., New York, N.Y. from: *Food and Drink:* a Pictorial Archive from 19th Century Sources, edited by Jim Harter, 1979; *Women:*, a Pictorial Archive from 19th Century Sources, edited by Jim Harter, 1978; and *Calligraphy:* by Johann George Schwanander, 1958.

Book Design and Lettering by Sigrid Andersen

ISBN 0-916870-59-6

Published by
CREATIVE ARTS COMMUNICATIONS
833 Bancroft Way, Berkeley, California 94701

CONTENTS.

LITTLE SINGING MAIDENS.

Little singing maidens-
  Bright and good and gay,
Sweeter in the morning
  And all throughout the day.

Little singing maidens-
  Sing about tempeh,
Salads, soups, and stir-fry's, too
  Sing the happy way.

INTRODUCING TEMPEH

WELCOME TO THE EXCITING WORLD OF TEMPEH COOKING. IF YOU KNOW A LITTLE ABOUT TEMPEH AND WOULD LIKE TO KNOW A LOT MORE, THIS BOOK WILL SHOW YOU MANY DELICIOUS WAYS TO PREPARE IT. IF YOU KNOW NOTHING AT ALL, YOU CAN LEARN ALL ABOUT IT RIGHT HERE.

TEMPEH IS MADE FROM SOYBEANS, OR FROM SOYBEANS COMBINED WITH GRAINS. IT IS FIRM AND MILD FLAVORED AND HAS THE TEXTURE OF TENDER CHICKEN BREAST OR VEAL. IT IS HIGH IN PROTEIN, LOW IN FAT, AND HAS NO CHOLESTEROL AT ALL. TEMPEH IS RICH IN VITAMIN B-12 AND IRON.

YOU CAN FIND TEMPEH IN MOST NATURAL FOOD STORES AND IN MANY GROCERY STORES, SOMETIMES IN THE FREEZER SECTION, SOMETIMES IN THE DAIRY CASE. IT IS USUALLY PACKAGED AS AN EIGHT OUNCE CAKE, THAT IS ABOUT 1/2 INCH THICK. YOU CAN ALSO BUY FLAVORED TEMPEH IN BURGERS OR CUTLETS.

TEMPEH IS A CULTURED FOOD, LIKE YOGURT OR CHEESE. IT IS MADE BY MIXING PARTIALLY COOKED SOYBEANS WITH A STARTER CULTURE. THE BEANS ARE PACKED INTO PERFORATED PLASTIC BAGS, PATTED INTO FLAT CAKES, AND ALLOWED

TO INCUBATE IN A WARM PLACE FOR ABOUT 30 HOURS. THE INCUBATION PROCESS TENDERIZES THE BEANS AND MAKES THEM EASY TO DIGEST. THE CULTURE USED TO MAKE TEMPEH ABSORBS THE RAFFINOSE: THE INDIGESTIBLE PART OF BEANS. (PEOPLE WHO HAVE HAD A PROBLEM WITH BEANS SHOULD NOT HAVE A PROBLEM WITH TEMPEH.) THE COOKING TIME IS SHORTENED TOO, FROM THREE HOURS FOR SOYBEANS TO FIFTEEN MINUTES FOR TEMPEH.

COMPARING TEMPEH TO OTHER PROTEIN FOODS

A QUANTITY OF 3 1/2 OZ.	CALORIES	PROTEIN (IN GRAMS)	FAT (IN GRAMS)	CHOLESTEROL (IN MGS.)	IRON (IN MGS.)	SODIUM (IN MGS.)
TEMPEH	149	18.3	4.0	0	10	Tr.
GROUND BEEF (22% FAT, RAW)	268	17.9	21.2	70	3.9	41
CHICKEN (NO SKIN)	104	23.3	.5	60	1.1	90
EGGS (2 LARGE)	163	12.9	11.5	550	1.1	59
HALIBUT (RAW)	155	20.9	1.2	70	1.2	54
TOFU	72	7.8	4.2	0	1.9	7

TEMPEH IS MADE FROM SOYBEANS ALONE OR FROM SOYBEANS MIXED WITH GRAINS SUCH AS RICE, WHEAT, BARLEY, OATS, AND MILLET. JUST AS BREAD GETS ITS FLAVOR FROM THE KIND OF FLOUR USED, THE FLAVOR OF TEMPEH CHANGES WITH THE BEANS AND

GRAINS FROM WHICH IT IS MADE. THE MOST DELICATELY FLAVORED TEMPEH IS MADE FROM A COMBINATION OF DIFFERENT GRAINS. THREE, FOUR, OR FIVE GRAIN TEMPEH EASILY ABSORBS THE FLAVORS OF WHATEVER IT IS COOKED WITH, AND GOES ESPECIALLY WELL WITH CREAM SAUCES AND CHEESE.

SOY-RICE TEMPEH HAS A MILD, MUSHROOM-LIKE FLAVOR THAT COMBINES WELL WITH MOST SEASONINGS. IT ADDS ITS OWN FLAVOR WITHOUT OVERWHELMING A DISH. PURE SOY TEMPEH HAS THE MOST DISTINCTIVE FLAVOR. IT DOES WELL IN HEARTY TOMATO SAUCES, MEXICAN DISHES, AND CURRIES.

TEMPEH BURGERS AND CUTLETS ARE PRE-SEASONED, USUALLY WITH SOY SAUCE, HERBS, AND SPICES. SOME ARE PRE-COOKED AND NEED ONLY WARMING; OTHERS ARE PARTIALLY COOKED, NEEDING ONLY FIVE TO EIGHT MINUTES ADDITIONAL COOKING. PRE-SEASONED TEMPEH BLENDS WELL WITH OTHER INGREDIENTS IN SOUPS, CASSEROLES, SALADS, AND STIR-FRY DISHES.

THE TYPE OF TEMPEH YOU PREFER IS REALLY UP TO YOU. KEEP SOME IN YOUR FREEZER FOR ALMOST INSTANT MEALS.

COOKING WITH TEMPEH IS EASY. IT CAN BE SAUTÉED, FRIED, STEAMED, BAKED, OR SIMMERED. IT CAN BE USED INSTEAD OF CHICKEN IN SALADS, CASSEROLES, SOUPS, SAUCES, AND STIR-FRY DISHES. THERE IS NO WASTE: NO BONES, NO SKIN, NO FAT, AND NO SHRINKAGE. BEST OF ALL, TEMPEH FREEZES WELL; IT WILL KEEP IN A FREEZER FROM 3 TO 6 MONTHS. IN HALF AN HOUR IT IS THAWED AND READY TO USE IN SO MANY QUICK, EASY, AND DELICIOUS WAYS!

TEMPEH CAN SUBSTITUTE FOR COOKED CHICKEN BREAST IN ANY RECIPE IF IT IS CUT INTO CUBES AND SIMMERED TEN TO FIFTEEN MINUTES IN A RICH SOUP STOCK. THE TEMPEH ABSORBS THE SOUP FLAVOR AND BECOMES MOIST AND TENDER. IT CAN ALSO BE STEAMED OVER BOILING WATER FOR TEN TO FIFTEEN MINUTES AND THEN COMBINED WITH A A MARINADE OR DRESSING. THIS WORKS ESPECIALLY WELL FOR COLD TEMPEH IN SALADS.

WHEN COATED WITH SEASONED FLOUR AND SHALLOW FRIED, TEMPEH DEVELOPS A TENDER CRUST. DEEP FRIED, IT IS LIKE FRIED CHICKEN. CUBED AND STIR-FRIED WITH GARLIC AND GINGER IT CAN BE USED INSTEAD, OF OR IN ADDITION TO, CHICKEN OR PORK IN YOUR FAVORITE CHINESE DISHES. TEMPEH CAN ALSO BE BAKED, ADDING TEXTURE, FLAVOR, AND NUTRITION TO ANY CASSEROLE.

MANY RECIPES IN THIS BOOK CALL FOR TEMPEH TO BE SERVED OVER RICE OR NOODLES. THERE ARE TWO REASONS FOR THIS. THE FLAVOR OF THE SAUCES GOES VERY WELL WITH THESE FOODS, BUT MORE IMPORTANTLY, WHEN TEMPEH IS COMBINED WITH GRAINS THE AMOUNT OF PROTEIN MADE AVAILABLE TO THE BODY IS INCREASED BY AS MUCH AS ONE THIRD. THE QUALITY OF THE PROTEIN IS EXACTLY THE SAME AS THAT DERIVED FROM MEATS AND EGGS.

EIGHT OUNCES OF TEMPEH GENERALLY YIELDS FOUR SERVINGS; TWO OUNCES PROVIDES OVER TEN GRAMS OF PROTEIN, ABOUT TWENTY PERCENT OF THE RECOMMENDED ADULT DAILY REQUIREMENT. BUT TEMPEH IS NOT EATEN ALONE. COMBINED WITH RICE OR WHEAT, VEGETABLES, AND PERHAPS A LITTLE MILK OR CHEESE, TWO OUNCES OF TEMPEH PROVIDES ONE THIRD OR MORE OF YOUR DAILY PROTEIN NEEDS.

TEMPEH CAN BE SERVED IN SO MANY WAYS THAT MEAL PLANNING IS A JOY. WITH THESE SAUCE, STEW, AND CASSEROLE RECIPES YOU NEED ONLY ADD A GREEN SALAD AND A COOKED VEGETABLE TO HAVE A SATISFYING AND NUTRITIOUS MEAL. THE SALADS PROVIDE THE BASIS FOR ANY LUNCH, AND CAN BE SERVED EITHER ON A BED OF GREENS OR AS A SANDWICH FILLING. THE SOUPS, SERVED WITH A SALAD AND A QUICK BREAD, MAKE A NOURISHING COLD WEATHER MEAL. THE STIR-FRY DISHES WILL ADD DIVERSITY AND EXTRA PROTEIN TO YOUR FAVORITE CHINESE PREPARATIONS.

TEMPEH IS SO EASY TO USE, SO VERSATILE, NUTRITIOUS, AND DELICIOUS THAT IT WILL WELL REWARD YOUR EFFORTS TO FIND IT! A FEW CAKES OF TEMPEH AND SOME BURGERS OR CUTLETS IN YOUR FREEZER MEANS AN UNLIMITED RANGE OF TASTY DISHES CAN BE ON YOUR TABLE IN A VERY SHORT TIME. DO ENJOY THE RECIPES IN THIS BOOK, AND THEN GO ON TO CREATE SOME OF YOUR OWN!

A WORD ABOUT SALT

TEMPEH HAS ONLY A TRACE OF SODIUM. IT IS POROUS, ABSORBING SOME OF THE LIQUID IT IS COOKED IN. IF YOU ARE CONCERNED WITH SODIUM BE SURE THE STOCK YOU USE IN COOKING TEMPEH IS NOT TOO SALTY. SALT CAN BE OMITTED OR CUT DOWN IN ANY RECIPE. IN MANY CASES IT IS BEST TO "SALT TO TASTE".

NOTES

SALADS AND SANDWICHES

U's a Unique Unicorn
Who always ate tempeh at dawn
He said he ate more
Than he e'er did before
But it made him feel rather new born.

WINTER SALAD

SERVES 4 TO 6

A WARM SALAD FOR A COLD WINTER'S NIGHT.

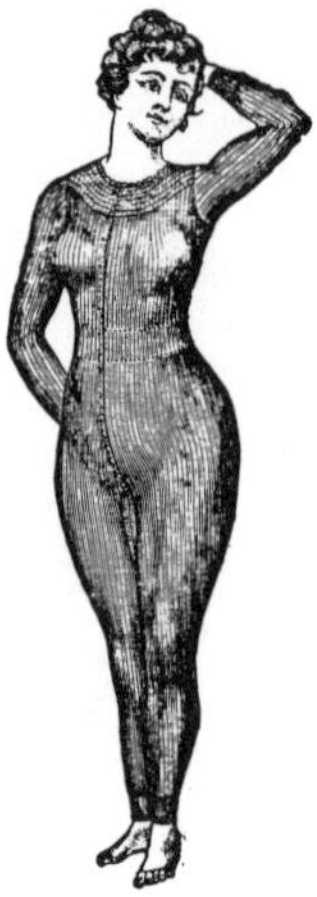

- 2 CARROTS, SLICED THIN
- 1 CUP CELERY, SLICED
- 1 SMALL ONION, CHOPPED
- 2 TBSP. SALAD OIL
- 8 OZ. TEMPEH, GRAIN OR SOY
- 1/2 CUP VEGETABLE OR CHICKEN STOCK
- 1/2 CUP MAYONNAISE
- SALT AND PEPPER TO TASTE
- 1 TSP. WORCESTERSHIRE SAUCE
- 2 GREEN ONION, CHOPPED (INCLUDING TOPS)

SAUTÉ CARROTS, CELERY, AND ONION IN OIL UNTIL ONION SOFTENS. CUT TEMPEH INTO 1/4 INCH CUBES. ADD THE TEMPEH TO VEGETABLES ALONG WITH THE STOCK AND SIMMER FOR 15 MINUTES. REMOVE TEMPEH AND VEGETABLES WITH A SLOTTED SPOON AND DISCARD REMAINING LIQUID. FOLD MAYONNAISE, SALT AND PEPPER (TO TASTE), AND WORCESTERSHIRE SAUCE INTO THE TEMPEH AND VEGETABLE SALAD. SPRINKLE WITH CHOPPED GREEN ONIONS AND SERVE WARM.

TEMPEH ROLLS

SERVES 4

7 TO 8 OZ. PRE-SEASONED TEMPEH (CUTLETS OR BURGERS)
1/2 CUP WATER OR STOCK
3 OZ. CREAM CHEESE
1/4 CUP CHOPPED CELERY
1/4 CUP CHOPPED CARROT
1/4 CUP CHOPPED RADISHES
SALT AND PEPPER TO TASTE
4 FRENCH ROLLS

CUT TEMPEH INTO 1/4 INCH CUBES AND SIMMER IN WATER OR STOCK 5 MINUTES. REMOVE FROM LIQUID WITH A SLOTTED SPOON AND SET ASIDE TO COOL.

MEASURE REMAINING LIQUID. BLEND 1/4 CUP INTO CREAM CHEESE AND BEAT UNTIL SMOOTH. ADD TEMPEH CUBES AND CHOPPED VEGETABLES. MIX WELL. ADD SALT AND PEPPER TO TASTE. REFRIGERATE UNTIL SERVING UNTIL SERVING TIME.

FILL HOLLOWED OUT FRENCH ROLLS WITH SALAD AND SERVE WARMED OR COLD.

CURRY SALAD

SERVES 4

7 TO 8 OZ. PRE-SEASONED TEMPEH
1 TBSP. SALAD OIL
2 STALKS CELERY, CHOPPED
1 CUP CUBED JICAMA (OR CUCUMBER)
2 GREEN ONIONS, SLICED
1 CUP SEEDLESS GRAPES, HALVED
CURRY DRESSING (SEE BELOW)
1 BUNCH SPINACH
1 CUP ALFALFA SPROUTS
TOASTED SUNFLOWER OR SESAME SEEDS

CUT TEMPEH INTO 1/4 INCH CUBES AND SAUTÉ IN OIL FOR 5 MINUTES, STIRRING OFTEN. SET ASIDE TO COOL.

COMBINE THE CELERY, JICAMA, GREEN ONION, AND HALVED GRAPES IN A SALAD BOWL. ADD THE TEMPEH CUBES AND CURRY DRESSING (SEE BELOW). STIR GENTLY AND CHILL AT LEAST 1 HOUR. TO SERVE, WASH AND TEAR THE SPINACH LEAVES INTO BITE SIZE PIECES. COMBINE WITH ALFALFA SPROUTS SPROUTS AND DIVIDE EVENLY AMONG 4 PLATES. TOP GREENS WITH CURRIED TEMPEH SALAD AND SPRINKLE WITH SEEDS.

CURRY DRESSING

2/3 CUP MAYONNAISE
2 TSP. CURRY POWDER
1/2 TSP. GROUND GINGER
1 TSP. SOY SAUCE
2 TSP. LEMON JUICE
2 TSP. HONEY

COMBINE ALL INGREDIENTS AND MIX UNTIL THOROUGHLY BLENDED.

CRUNCHY-TOP SALAD

REALLY DELICIOUS!

SERVES 4 TO 6

8 OZ. TEMPEH, GRAIN OR SOY
1/2 CUP FRENCH DRESSING
1/2 CUP MAYONNAISE
1/2 CUP PLAIN YOGURT
1 1/2 CUPS DICED CELERY
1/4 CUP TOASTED SLIVERED ALMONDS
2 CUPS FINELY CRUSHED POTATO CHIPS
1 CUP GRATED CHEESE

CUT TEMPEH INTO 1/4 INCH CUBES AND STEAM OVER BOILING WATER FOR 10 MINUTES. REMOVE FROM STEAMER TO A MEDIUM SIZE MIXING BOWL. ADD THE FRENCH DRESSING. STIR GENTLY AND MARINATE FOR 1 HOUR. MIX THE MAYONNAISE AND THE YOGURT UNTIL CREAMY; ADD THE CELERY AND SLIVERED ALMONDS AND MIX WELL. STIR INTO MARINATED TEMPEH AND CHILL.

ABOUT 15 MINUTES BEFORE SERVING, SPREAD INTO A 7×11 INCH PAN. MIX THE CRUSHED POTATO CHIPS AND CHEESE AND COMPLETELY COVER THE TEMPEH SALAD. BROIL UNTIL BROWNED AND CRUNCHY!

SERVE IMMEDIATELY!

PASTA TWIST SALAD

SERVES 4 TO 6

- 4 OZ. PASTA TWISTS
- 8 OZ. TEMPEH, GRAIN OR SOY
- 1/2 CUP VEGETABLE OR CHICKEN STOCK
- 1 MILD ONION, CHOPPED FINE
- 2 MEDIUM TOMATOES, CHOPPED
- 1 SMALL GREEN PEPPER, CHOPPED
- 4 OZ. SLICED OLIVES (1 CAN)
- 2 TBSP. FRESH CHOPPED PARSLEY
- 2 TO 3 STALKS CELERY, CHOPPED

COOK PASTA TWIST, SET ASIDE TO COOL. CUT TEMPEH INTO QUARTERS, PUT IN A MEDIUM SKILLET WITH THE STOCK AND BRING TO A BOIL. COVER AND SIMMER 3 MINUTES. TURN TEMPEH OVER AND SIMMER 5 MINUTES MORE. REMOVE TEMPEH, COOL, AND CUT INTO 1/4 INCH CUBES. COMBINE WITH THE CHOPPED ONION, TOMATOES, GREEN PEPPERS, OLIVES, PARSLEY, AND CELERY. SET ASIDE.

DRESSING

- 1/3 CUP WINE VINEGAR
- 1/2 CUP OLIVE OIL
- 1/2 CUP MAYONNAISE
- 1/2 TSP. DRIED BASIL, CRUMBLED
- SALT AND PEPPER TO TASTE

BLEND THE VINEGAR, OIL, MAYONNAISE, BASIL, SALT, AND PEPPER WELL. POUR OVER TEMPEH AND VEGETABLES. ADD COOKED PASTA TWISTS AND TOSS GENTLY. CHILL FOR AT LEAST 1 HOUR BEFORE SERVING. KEEPS WELL FOR SEVERAL DAYS WHEN REFRIGERATED.

MOCK CHICKEN SALAD

SERVES 4

8 OZ. TEMPEH, GRAIN OR SOY
1 CUP VEGETABLE OR CHICKEN STOCK
1/3 CUP MAYONNAISE
1/3 CUP SOUR CREAM OR YOGURT
1 TBSP. LEMON JUICE
1/4 TSP. PEPPER
3/4 CUP CHOPPED CELERY
1 BUNCH GREEN ONIONS, SLICED
1/4 CUP CHOPPED DILL PICKLE
- LETTUCE
- PAPRIKA

CUT TEMPEH INTO 1/4 INCH CUBES AND SIMMER IN STOCK FOR 10 MINUTES. REMOVE WITH A SLOTTED SPOON AND LET COOL.

BLEND MAYONNAISE, SOUR CREAM, LEMON JUICE, PEPPER, CELERY, GREEN ONION, AND DILL PICKLE. STIR IN TEMPEH CUBES AND TOSS GENTLY. ADD SALT TO TASTE. COVER AND CHILL FOR AT LEAST 1 HOUR.

SERVE SALAD IN A LETTUCE LINED BOWL. SPRINKLE WITH PAPRIKA.

DEVILED TEMPEH

SERVES 2 TO 3

- 7 TO 8 OZ. PRESEASONED TEMPEH (CUTLETS OR BURGERS)
- 1 TBSP. SALAD OIL
- 1/2 CUP DICED CELERY
- 2 OR 3 GREEN ONIONS, SLICED THIN
- 4 TBSP. MAYONNAISE
- 1 TBSP. MILK
- 2 TO 3 TSP. PREPARED MUSTARD
- SALT TO TASTE
- 2 OR 3 FRENCH, ONION, OR KAISER ROLLS

SAUTÉ TEMPEH IN OIL, ON EACH SIDE, UNTIL BROWNED AND CRISP. COOL AND CUT INTO 1/4 INCH CUBES. COMBINE TEMPEH, CELERY, AND GREEN ONIONS IN A MEDIUM BOWL. MIX MAYONNAISE, MILK AND MUSTARD AND ADD TO THE TEMPEH MIXTURE, STIRRING GENTLY. SALT TO TASTE AND CHILL UNTIL SERVING TIME.

SLICE THE ROLLS IN HALF AND SPOON ON THE DEVILED TEMPEH. BROIL 2 TO 3 MINUTES, UNTIL EDGES OF ROLLS ARE CRISP.

DEVILISHLY GOOD!

PATÉ TEMPEH

MAKES 2 CUPS

PATE DE FOIE TEMPEH!

1 CUP SLIVERED ALMONDS
1 SMALL ONION, MINCED
1 CLOVE GARLIC, MINCED
1/2 LB. SLICED MUSHROOMS
4 TBSP. BUTTER OR MARGARINE
8 OZ. TEMPEH, GRAIN OR SOY
SALT TO TASTE
1/4 TSP. LEAF THYME
1/8 TSP. LEAF SAGE
1 TBSP. SOY SAUCE
2 TBSP. SALAD OIL

TOAST THE ALMONDS IN A 325° OVEN FOR 15 TO 20 MINUTES, UNTIL THEY ARE GOLDEN BROWN. SET ASIDE TO COOL. SAUTÉ THE ONION, GARLIC, AND, MUSHROOMS IN BUTTER OR MARGARINE UNTIL SOFTENED. CUT TEMPEH INTO 1/2 INCH CUBES AND ADD TO THE MUSHROOM MIXTURE. ADD THE SALT, THYME, SAGE, AND SOY SAUCE. COOK, STIRRING OFTEN, UNTIL MOST OF THE LIQUID HAS COOKED OUT - ABOUT 15 MINUTES.

IN A FOOD PROCESSOR OR BLENDER, GRIND THE ALMONDS TO A FINE POWDER. ADD OIL AND PROCESS UNTIL A THICK NUT BUTTER FORMS. ADD THE TEMPEH MIXTURE 1/2 CUP AT A TIME, AND PROCESS UNTIL THE PATÉ IS THICK AND SMOOTH. ADD MORE SALT, IF NEEDED. KEEPS, REFRIGERATED, FOR ABOUT A WEEK.

NOTES

SOUP AND STIR-FRY

R, was a Rowdy young Rabbit
Who had a most terrible habit!
When he saw any tempeh
Whatever one might say
He'd rise from his chair,
and just grab it.

MULLIGATAWNY SOUP

SERVES 6

3 MEDIUM CARROTS, SLICED
2 STALKS CELERY, SLICED
6 CUPS VEGETABLE OR CHICKEN STOCK
8 OZ. TEMPEH, GRAIN OR SOY
1 LARGE ONION, CHOPPED
4 TBSP. BUTTER OR MARGARINE
1 LARGE APPLE, PEELED AND CHOPPED
1 TO 2 TBSP. CURRY POWDER
1 TSP. SALT (OR TO TASTE)
1/4 CUP FLOUR
1 TO 2 TBSP. LEMON JUICE
2 TO 3 CUPS HOT COOKED RICE
1/2 CUP CHOPPED ROASTED PEANUTS (OPTIONAL)

COOK SLICED CARROTS AND CELERY IN 1 CUP STOCK FOR 5 MINUTES. CUT TEMPEH INTO 1/4 INCH CUBES, ADD TO STOCK AND SIMMER 5 MINUTES MORE. REMOVE FROM HEAT.

SAUTÉ ONION UNTIL SOFT IN BUTTER OR MARGARINE IN A LARGE SOUP POT OR DUTCH OVEN. ADD CHOPPED APPLE, CURRY POWDER, SALT AND FLOUR AND SAUTE FOR 3 MINUTES, STIRRING CONSTANTLY. GRADUALLY ADD THE REMAINING STOCK AND HEAT TO BOILING, STIRRING OFTEN. REDUCE HEAT, ADD TEMPEH AND VEGETABLES, COVER AND SIMMER FOR 10 MINUTES. REMOVE FROM HEAT AND STIR IN LEMON JUICE.

PUT ABOUT 1/2 CUP RICE IN EACH SOUP BOWL. POUR SOUP OVER RICE AND GARNISH WITH CHOPPED PEANUTS. DELICIOUS!

TARRAGON SOUP

SERVES 4 TO 6

7 TO 8 OZ. PRE-SEASONED TEMPEH (CUTLETS OR BURGERS)
1/2 CUP FINELY CHOPPED CELERY
2 TBSP. BUTTER OR MARGARINE
5 CUPS VEGETABLE OR CHICKEN STOCK
1/4 CUP DRY WHITE WINE (OPTIONAL)
1/8 TSP. PEPPER
SALT TO TASTE
1 TSP. LEAF TARRAGON, CRUMBLED
1 PACKAGE (10 OZ.) FROZEN PEAS (THAWED)
3 GREEN ONIONS, SLICED THIN (INCLUDING TOPS)

CUT TEMPEH INTO 1/4 INCH CUBES. SAUTE TEMPEH AND CELERY IN BUTTER OR MARGARINE 3 MINUTES. ADD STOCK, WINE, PEPPER, SALT, AND TARRAGON. BRING TO A BOIL, THEN SIMMER 10 MINUTES. ADD THAWED PEAS AND SIMMER 5 MINUTES MORE.

GARNISH WITH SLICED GREEN ONIONS AND SERVE.

TENDER DUMPLINGS

MAKES ABOUT 16 DUMPLINGS

7 TO 8 OZ. PRE-SEASONED TEMPEH (CUTLETS OR BURGERS)
1 EGG
1/2 CUP MILK
DASH OF PEPPER
DASH OF NUTMEG
1 CUP WHOLE WHEAT FLOUR
1 TSP. BAKING POWDER
1/2 TSP. SALT (OR TO TASTE)
3 TO 4 CUPS VEGETABLE OR CHICKEN STOCK
2 TBSP. BUTTER OR MARGARINE
2 TBSP. FLOUR
1 TSP. WORCESTERSHIRE SAUCE

GRATE, CRUMBLE OR CHOP TEMPEH INTO SMALL PIECES. PUT TEMPEH, EGG, MILK, PEPPER, AND NUTMEG IN A BLENDER OR FOOD PROCESSOR AND PROCESS UNTIL SMOOTH. TURN OUT INTO A BOWL. SIFT TOGETHER THE FLOUR, BAKING POWDER, AND SALT. STIR INTO THE TEMPEH MIXTURE MIXTURE UNTIL A VERY THICK BATTER FORMS.

CONTINUED NEXT PAGE...

DUMPLINGS, CONT.

BRING STOCK TO A BOIL IN A MEDIUM SKILLET (AT LEAST 3 INCHES DEEP). SPOON ROUNDED TABLESPOONS OF BATTER OF INTO THE STOCK. DO NOT CROWD THE PAN. THE DUMPLINGS SHOULD HAVE PLENTY OF ROOM TO EXPAND WITHOUT TOUCHING. COVER SKILLET AND SIMMER DUMPLINGS 5 MINUTES. TURN DUMPLINGS OVER SIMMER, UNCOVERED, FOR 4 MORE MINUTES. REMOVE WITH A SLOTTED SPOON TO A HEATPROOF CASSEROLE AND KEEP WARM. IT WILL PROBABLY BE NECESSARY TO MAKE 3 BATCHES OF DUMPLINGS.

WHEN ALL DUMPLINGS ARE DONE, POUR STOCK OUT OF PAN AND MEASURE. ADD MILK TO MAKE 2 CUPS. RINSE PAN AND WIPE DRY. MELT THE BUTTER OR MARGARINE AND STIR IN FLOUR. COOK, STIRRING CONSTANTLY, TO MAKE A THICK WHITE SAUCE. BRING SAUCE TO A BOIL, THEN SIMMER 5 MINUTES. ADD WORCESTERSHIRE AND ADDITIONAL SALT AND PEPPER IF NEEDED. POUR SAUCE OVER DUMPLINGS, REHEAT IF NECESSARY, AND SERVE.

DUMPLINGS CAN ALSO BE COOKED IN, OR ADDED TO ANY SOUP FOR A DELICIOUS TREAT!

PEPPER TEMPEH

SERVES 4

8 OZ. TEMPEH, GRAIN OR SOY
1 TBSP. SOY SAUCE
1 TBSP. SHERRY OR RICE WINE
2 TBSP. CORNSTARCH
OIL FOR DEEP FRYING
1 ONION
1 MEDIUM CUCUMBER
2 GREEN BELL PEPPERS
1 SWEET RED PEPPER
1 GREEN CHILI PEPPER
3 TBSP. SOY SAUCE
1 TSP. HONEY
1 CUP VEGETABLE OR CHICKEN STOCK
2 TBSP. CORNSTARCH

CUT TEMPEH INTO 1 INCH CUBES. COMBINE SOY SAUCE, SHERRY, AND 2 TBSP. CORNSTARCH THOROUGHLY. ADD MIXTURE TO TEMPEH AND MIX GENTLY TO COAT THE TEMPEH AND LET STAND 20 MINUTES.

CONTINUED NEXT PAGE →

PEPPER, CONT.

CUT ONION INTO 1 INCH CHUNKS AND SEPARATE ONION LAYERS. PEEL CUCUMBER, CUT IN HALF LENGTHWISE, THEN INTO 1/2 INCH SLICES. SEED ALL PEPPERS AND CUT INTO 1 INCH CUBES EXCEPT FOR CHILI PEPPER, WHICH GETS FINELY CHOPPED. PUT 1 INCH OF OIL IN A WOK OR DEEP MEDIUM SKILLET AND HEAT. FRY THE TEMPEH CUBES UNTIL GOLDEN AND CRISPY. REMOVE AND DRAIN ON PAPER TOWELS. POUR OUT ALL BUT 2 TBSP. OIL AND STIR-FRY THE ONION, CUCUMBER, AND PEPPERS FOR 4 TO 5 MINUTES. REMOVE VEGETABLES FROM FRYING PAN AND SET ASIDE.

MIX 3 TBSP. SOY SAUCE, HONEY, 1 CUP STOCK, AND 2 TBSP. CORNSTARCH TOGETHER IN A SMALL BOWL. ADD MIXTURE TO WOK (OR SKILLET) AND BRING TO A BOIL, STIRRING CONSTANTLY, FOR 2 MINUTES OR UNTIL THICKENED. ADD TEMPEH AND SIMMER FOR 3 MINUTES. ADD THE VEGETABLES AND STIR UNTIL HEATED THROUGH AND COATED WITH SAUCE AND SERVE!

ALMOND STIR-FRY

SERVES 4

7 TO 8 OZ. PRE-SEASONED TEMPEH (CUTLETS OR BURGERS)
1 TBSP. WATER
1 TBSP. SOY SAUCE
1 TSP. HONEY
1 TBSP. CORNSTARCH
4 TBSP. SALAD OIL
1 CUP DICED CELERY
1 CUP DICED ONION
1 CUP CANNED BAMBOO SHOOTS, SLICED
8 WATER CHESTNUTS, SLICED
1/2 CUP VEGETABLE OR CHICKEN STOCK
1 TO 2 TBSP. SOY SAUCE
2 TBSP. SHERRY OR RICE WINE
1/2 CUP WHOLE, BLANCHED, AND ROASTED ALMONDS

CUT TEMPEH INTO 1/4 INCH CUBES. BEAT: WATER, SOY SAUCE, HONEY, AND CORNSTARCH TO MAKE A THICK PASTE. MIX WITH TEMPEH, STIRRING GENTLY TO COAT AS MUCH AS POSSIBLE. SET ASIDE.

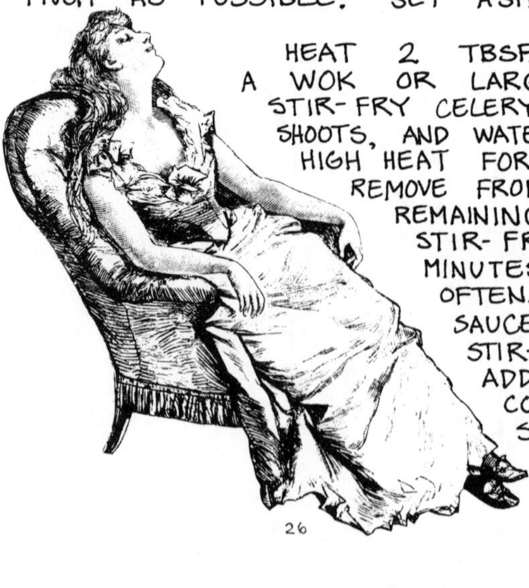

HEAT 2 TBSP. OF THE OIL IN A WOK OR LARGE SKILLET. STIR-FRY CELERY, ONION, BAMBOO SHOOTS, AND WATER CHESTNUTS OVER HIGH HEAT FOR 3 MINUTES. REMOVE FROM PAN. ADD REMAINING 2 TBSP. OIL. STIR-FRY TEMPEH FOR 3 MINUTES, STIRRING OFTEN. ADD STOCK, SOY SAUCE, SHERRY AND STIR-FRY 1 MINUTE. ADD VEGETABLES AND COOK 2 MINUTES. SPRINKLE ALMONDS ON TOP AND SERVE.

PEA-MUSHROOM STIR-FRY

SERVES 4

7 TO 8 OZ. PRE-SEASONED TEMPEH
3 TBSP. SALAD OIL
2 GREEN ONIONS
1 TSP. GRATED FRESH GINGER ROOT
1 CLOVE GARLIC, MINCED
6 TO 8 MEDIUM MUSHROOMS, SLICED
1 PKG. FROZEN PETITE PEAS, THAWED
1 CUP VEGETABLE OR CHICKEN STOCK
2 TBSP. SOY SAUCE
1 TBSP. SHERRY
1 TSP. HONEY
1/2 TSP. SALT (OR TO TASTE)
1 TBSP. CORNSTARCH OR ARROWROOT
2 TBSP. WATER

CUT TEMPEH INTO 1/4 INCH CUBES. HEAT OIL IN A WOK OR LARGE SKILLET AND STIR-FRY FOR 3 MINUTES. REMOVE FROM PAN AND SET ASIDE. CUT GREEN ONIONS INTO 1/4 INCH DIAGONAL SLICES, INCLUDING TOPS. ADD ALONG WITH GINGER AND GARLIC TO THE WOK AND STIR-FRY ABOUT 30 SECONDS. ADD MUSHROOMS AND STIR-FRY 2 MINUTES. ADD PEAS AND AND COOK 1 MINUTE MORE.

STIR TOGETHER STOCK, SOY SAUCE, SHERRY, HONEY, AND SALT. ADD TO MUSHROOMS AND PEAS AND BRING TO A SIMMER. ADD TEMPEH CUBES AND SIMMER 10 MINUTES. DISSOLVE CORNSTARCH OR ARROWROOT IN 2 TBSP. WATER AND ADD TO WOK. SIMMER, STIRRING ABOUT 2 MINUTES, UNTIL SAUCE HAS THICKENED. SERVE WITH STEAMED RICE.

CRISPY FRIED TEMPEH IN

SERVES 4

8 OZ. TEMPEH, SOY OR GRAIN
1 TBSP. SOY SAUCE
1 TBSP. SHERRY
1 CLOVE GARLIC, MINCED
1 TBSP. FRESH GINGER ROOT, GRATED
3 TO 4 TBSP. CORNSTARCH
1 SMALL BELL PEPPER
1 MEDIUM ONION
20 OZ. PINEAPPLE CHUNKS (1 CAN)
1 CUP OIL

SAUCE INGREDIENTS

1 1/2 TBSP. CORNSTARCH
1 TBSP. SOY SAUCE
2 TBSP. HONEY OR BROWN SUGAR
2 TBSP. VINEGAR
2 TBSP. CATSUP
1 CUP PINEAPPLE JUICE (FROM CHUNKS)

CUT THE TEMPEH INTO 3/4 INCH CUBES. MARINATE IN A MIXTURE OF THE SOY SAUCE, SHERRY, GARLIC, AND GINGER FOR FOR 20 MINUTES, STIRRING OCCASIONALLY. PUT THE CORNSTARCH INTO A SIFTER OR SMALL STRAINER AND DUST THE TEMPEH CUBES THOROUGHLY. PUT THEM ON A PLATE IN A SINGLE LAYER AND LET STAND AT LEAST 10 MINUTES.

CONTINUED NEXT PAGE...

SWEET AND SOUR SAUCE

CUT THE BELL PEPPER AND ONION INTO 1 INCH PIECES. SEPARATE THE ONION LAYERS. DRAIN THE JUICE FROM THE PINEAPPLE, MEASURE, AND ADD WATER IF NECESSARY TO MAKE 1 CUP. MIX THE CORNSTARCH, SOY SAUCE, HONEY, VINEGAR, CATSUP, AND PINEAPPLE JUICE TO MAKE THE SAUCE AND SET ASIDE.

HEAT 1 CUP OF OIL IN A WOK OR FRYING PAN. ADD TEMPEH CUBES ONE AT A TIME IN A SINGLE LAYER. DON'T CROWD THEM. BROWN TEMPEH ON ONE SIDE, TURN AND CONTINUE FRYING UNTIL BROWN AND CRISP. REMOVE TEMPEH TO PAPER TOWELS TO DRAIN. REMOVE ALL BUT 1 TBSP. OIL FROM THE WOK OR FRYING PAN. STIR-FRY PEPPERS AND ONIONS OVER HIGH HEAT FOR 2 MINUTES. ADD PINEAPPLE AND SAUCE INGREDIENTS. COOK 2 MINUTES MINUTES MORE, UNTIL THICKENED. STIR IN TEMPEH PIECES AND HEAT 1 MINUTE. SERVE ON A BED OF STEAMED RICE.

NOTES

STOVE TOP

L, was a Lively old Lion,
Whose conduct no man could rely on.
For he'd smile and look sweet
As the tempeh he'd eat,
And be thinking which person to fly on!

HUNGARIAN GOULASH

SERVES 4

THIS TASTES EVEN BETTER THE NEXT DAY!

- 2 CARROTS
- 1 GREEN PEPPER
- 2 STALKS CELERY
- 1 LARGE ONION
- 2 OR 3 RED POTATOES
- 2 TBSP. SALAD OIL
- 8 OZ. TOMATO SAUCE (1 CAN)
- 1 CUP WATER
- 1 BAY LEAF
- 8 OZ. TEMPEH, GRAIN OR SOY
- 1 TBSP. SWEET PAPRIKA
- 1 TSP. SALT
- 1 CUP SOUR CREAM OR PLAIN YOGURT

PEEL AND SLICE CARROTS 1/4 INCH THICK. REMOVE SEEDS AND CUT GREEN PEPPER INTO 1 INCH SQUARES, SLICE CELERY 1/4 INCH THICK AND COARSELY CHOP THE ONION. SCRUB BUT DO NOT PEEL THE POTATOES AND CUT INTO 1 INCH PIECES. SAUTÉ THE CARROTS, GREEN PEPPER, CELERY, ONION, AND POTATOES IN THE OIL FOR 5 MINUTES. ADD THE TOMATO SAUCE, WATER AND BAY LEAF, COVER AND SIMMER FOR 10 MINUTES.

CONTINUED . . .

GOULASH, CONTINUED

CUT THE TEMPEH INTO 1/2 INCH CUBES. ADD THE TEMPEH, PAPRIKA AND SALT TO THE VEGETABLE MIXTURE AND STIR GENTLY. COVER THE POT AND SIMMER 15 MINUTES MORE OR JUST UNTIL VEGETABLES ARE TENDER. REMOVE FROM HEAT. SLOWLY ADD THE SOUR CREAM OR YOGURT TO THE GOULASH, STIRRING CONSTANTLY.

REHEAT IF NECESSARY, AND SERVE WITH A HEARTY RED WINE.

TEMPEH MEXICANO

THIS RECIPE MAKES ABOUT 4 CUPS OF THICK, SPICY FILLING FOR TACOS, BURRITOS OR ENCHILADAS.

8 OZ. TEMPEH, GRAIN OR SOY
1 SMALL ONION, CHOPPED
2 TBSP. SALAD OIL
8 OZ. TOMATO SAUCE
4 OZ. PRE-COOKED, DICED GREEN CHILIS (1 CAN)
4 OZ. CHOPPED OLIVES
1/2 CUP SOUR CREAM
SALT TO TASTE
MEXICAN STYLE HOT SAUCE TO TASTE

CUT THE TEMPEH INTO 1/4 INCH CUBES AND PLACE IN A STEAMER BASKET. BRING 1 INCH OF WATER TO A BOIL IN A MEDIUM SAUCEPAN, ADD STEAMER BASKET, COVER PAN AND SIMMER FOR 10 MINUTES.

SAUTE THE ONIONS IN OIL UNTIL SOFTENED. ADD TOMATO SAUCE, GREEN CHILIS AND OLIVES. BRING TO A SIMMER. ADD THE STEAMED TEMPEH, STIRRING GENTLY. COVER AND SIMMER FOR 5 MINUTES. REMOVE FROM HEAT AND SLOWLY ADD THE SOUR CREAM, STIRRING GENTLY BUT THOROUGHLY. ADD SALT AND HOT SAUCE TO TASTE.

¡OLE!

CASHEW CURRY

SERVES 5 TO 6

THIS IS GREAT THE NEXT DAY TOO!

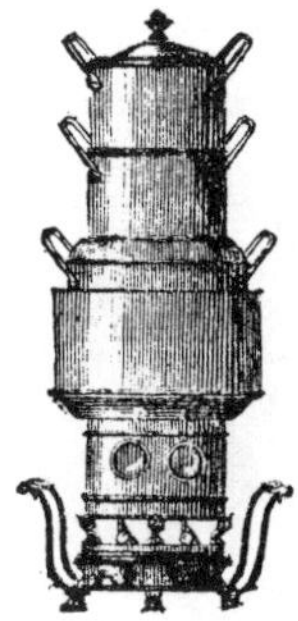

4 TBSP. BUTTER OR MARGARINE
1 SMALL ONION, CHOPPED
8 OZ. TEMPEH, GRAIN OR SOY
1 CUP SLICED MUSHROOMS
SALT AND PEPPER TO TASTE
1 TBSP. CURRY POWDER
1 CUP RAW WHITE OR BROWN RICE
2 1/2 CUPS VEGETABLE OR CHICKEN STOCK
2 MEDIUM TOMATOES
1/2 CUP ROASTED CASHEW NUTS
2 TBSP. CHOPPED FRESH PARSLEY (OR 1 TSP. DRIED PARSLEY)

MELT FAT IN A LARGE SKILLET. ADD ONION AND SAUTÉ OVER MEDIUM HEAT UNTIL THEY BEGIN TO SOFTEN. CUT TEMPEH INTO 1/2 INCH CUBES. ADD TEMPEH AND MUSHROOMS TO THE SKILLET AND SAUTÉ UNTIL MUSHROOMS SOFTEN. THEN ADD SALT, PEPPER, CURRY POWDER, AND RICE. COOK FOR 5 MINUTES STIRRING FREQUENTLY.

HEAT THE STOCK. PEEL AND CHOP THE TOMATOES. ADD BOTH TO THE SKILLET; STIR GENTLY, AND BRING TO A SIMMER; COVER AND COOK OVER LOW HEAT FOR 20 MINUTES. LIQUID SHOULD BE COMPLETELY ABSORBED AND THE RICE TENDER. REMOVE FROM HEAT AND LET STAND FOR 5 MINUTES. STIR IN THE CASHEWS AND PARSLEY JUST BEFORE SERVING.

CHICKEN AND TEMPEH

SERVES 6

TEMPEH AND GARLIC COULD BE LOVERS - THEY GO SO WELL TOGETHER

8 OZ. TEMPEH
1 LB. BONED AND SKINNED CHICKEN
1/4 CUP OIL
1/4 TO 1 TSP. CAYENNE PEPPER (TO TASTE)
5 TO 10 CLOVES GARLIC
1/3 CUP HONEY
1 1/4 CUP VINEGAR
1/3 CUP SOY SAUCE
2 TSP. CORNSTARCH
2 TSP. ROASTED PEANUTS OR SESAME SEEDS

CUT TEMPEH AND CHICKEN INTO 1 INCH CUBES. HEAT 2 TABLESPOONS OF OIL IN A SKILLET AND COOK THE CHICKEN UNTIL BROWNED AND TENDER. REMOVE WITH A SLOTTED SPOON AND SET ASIDE. ADD THE REST OF THE OIL, HEAT AND BROWN THE TEMPEH. CHOP THE GARLIC, COARSELY, AND ADD TO THE TEMPEH WITH THE PEPPER. ADD THE COOKED CHICKEN MEAT. COMBINE THE HONEY, VINEGAR, SOY SAUCE, CORNSTARCH AND MIX WELL. ADD THIS TO THE SKILLET AND STIR TO COAT ALL PIECES OF CHICKEN AND TEMPEH. COOK, STIRRING OFTEN, FOR ABOUT 10 MINUTES POUR INTO A SERVING BOWL AND SPRINKLE WITH NUTS.

HUNTER'S STEW

SERVES 4

1 LARGE ONION
3 STALKS CELERY
2 CARROTS
8 TO 10 MUSHROOMS
1 LARGE CLOVE GARLIC, PEELED
2 TBSP. SALAD OIL
8 OZ. TEMPEH, GRAIN OR SOY
1/2 CUP RED WINE
8 OZ. TOMATO SAUCE (1 CAN)
1 TSP. WORCESTERSHIRE SAUCE
SALT TO TASTE
1 BAY LEAF
1 TSP. OREGANO
1/4 TSP. THYME

CHOP THE ONION, COARSELY, CUT CELERY INTO 1/2 INCH SLICES AND CARROTS INTO 1/4 INCH SLICES. CUT THE LARGER MUSHROOMS IN HALF, LEAVE SMALLER ONES WHOLE. SAUTÉ ONION, CELERY, CARROTS, MUSHROOMS AND GARLIC IN OIL IN A LARGE SKILLET FOR 2 MINUTES CUT THE TEMPEH INTO 1/2 INCH CUBES AND ADD TO THE VEGETABLES. SAUTÉ 5 MINUTES MORE, UNTIL ONION IS SOFT AND TEMPEH IS SLIGHTLY BROWNED.

ADD RED WINE AND TOMATO SAUCE ALONG WITH THE WORCESTERSHIRE SAUCE, SALT (TO TASTE), BAY LEAF, OREGANO AND THYME. COVER AND SIMMER 20 MINUTES, STIRRING OCCASIONALLY. IF VEGETABLES ARE NOT SOFT ENOUGH CONTINUE SIMMERING UNTIL THEY ARE. IF THE SAUCE IS TOO THICK ADD SOME WATER OR MORE RED WINE. REMOVE GARLIC AND BAY LEAF BEFORE SERVING. SERVE OVER RICE OR WIDE COOKED NOODLES.

MEDITERRANEAN STEW

SERVES 4 TO 6

TEMPEH GOES TO THE SOUTH OF FRANCE!

8 OZ. TEMPEH, GRAIN OR SOY
4 TBSP. OLIVE OR SALAD OIL
1 MEDIUM ONION, CHOPPED
1 CLOVE GARLIC, MINCED
1 MEDIUM EGGPLANT
1 SMALL ZUCCHINI
2 MEDIUM TOMATOES
8 OZ. TOMATO SAUCE
1/2 CUP RED WINE OR WATER
SALT AND PEPPER TO TASTE
1 TSP. BASIL
1/2 TSP. OREGANO
1/4 CUP GRATED PARMESAN OR ROMANO CHEESE

CUT TEMPEH INTO 1/2 INCH CUBES AND BROWN LIGHTLY IN 3 TBSP. OIL IN A LARGE SKILLET. REMOVE FROM PAN AND SET ASIDE. PEEL THE EGGPLANT, IF DESIRED, AND CUT INTO 1 INCH CUBES. CUT ZUCCHINI IN HALF, LENGTHWISE, AND THEN INTO 1/2 INCH SLICES. PEEL AND COARSELY CHOP THE TOMATOES.

ADD REMAINING OIL TO SKILLET AND SAUTÉ ONION AND GARLIC UNTIL SOFTENED. ADD EGGPLANT, ZUCCHINI, TOMATOES, TOMATO SAUCE AND WINE. STIR IN SEASONINGS AND THE TEMPEH CUBES. COVER AND SIMMER FOR 25 MINUTES OR UNTIL THE VEGETABLES ARE SOFT. SPRINKLE WITH CHEESE BEFORE SERVING.

APPLE TEMPEH SAUTÉ

SERVES 4

8 OZ. TEMPEH, GRAIN OR SOY
2 TBSP. BUTTER OR MARGARINE
1 SMALL ONION, MINCED
1/4 LB. MUSHROOMS, SLICED
1 PEELED APPLE, CHOPPED
1 TBSP. CHOPPED FRESH PARSLEY
1/2 TSP. SEASONED SALT
1/4 TSP. THYME
1/8 TSP. ROSEMARY
1 CUP APPLE JUICE
1 TBSP. ARROWROOT
1/2 CUP LIGHT CREAM

CUT TEMPEH INTO STRIPS 1/4 INCH WIDE AND 2 INCHES LONG. MELT FAT IN A MEDIUM SKILLET; SAUTÉ ONION, MUSHROOMS, AND APPLE  UNTIL SOFTENED. ADD TEMPEH STRIPS AND GENTLY SAUTE 5 MINUTES, UNTIL ALL LIQUID IS ABSORBED AND TEMPEH IS LIGHTLY BROWNED. STIR IN THE SALT, (IF DESIRED) PARSLEY, THYME, ROSEMARY, AND APPLE JUICE. COVER AND SIMMER FOR 15 MINUTES.

REMOVE TEMPEH WITH A SLOTTED SPOON AND SET ASIDE. STIR ARROWROOT INTO CREAM AND ADD TO SKILLET. COOK OVER LOW HEAT, STIRRING CONSTANTLY, UNTIL SAUCE BOILS AND THICKENS. RETURN TEMPEH TO SAUCE TO HEAT THROUGH. SERVE WITH RICE OR OVEN FRIES.

SKILLET TEMPEH ITALIANO

SERVES 4 TO 6

8 OZ. TEMPEH, GRAIN OR SOY
1/2 CUP FLOUR
SALT AND PEPPER TO TASTE
4 TBSP. OLIVE OR SALAD OIL
2 LARGE ONIONS
1 LARGE CLOVE GARLIC
1/4 LB. MUSHROOMS
2 MEDIUM GREEN PEPPERS
28 OZ. STEWED ITALIAN TOMATOES
1 TSP. HONEY
1 TSP. BASIL
1/2 TSP. OREGANO
COOKED NOODLES OR SPAGHETTI

CUT TEMPEH INTO 1 INCH CUBES AND SHAKE IN A PAPER BAG WITH FLOUR, SALT AND PEPPER. BROWN TEMPEH CUBES LIGHTLY IN 3 TBSP. OIL IN A LARGE SKILLET. REMOVE TEMPEH WHEN BROWNED AND DRAIN ON A PAPER TOWEL.

PEEL THE ONIONS, CUT IN HALF, LENGTHWISE, AND SLICE 1/8 INCH THICK. MINCE THE GARLIC. CLEAN MUSHROOMS AND CUT IN HALF. HALVE, SEED AND CUT THE GREEN PEPPERS INTO 1/8 INCH SLICES.

No. 6.

CONTINUED...

No. 5.

No. 1.

No. 2.

No. 3.

No. 4.

ITALIANO, CONTINUED

ADD REMAINING 1 TBSP. OIL TO THE SKILLET AND SAUTE THE ONION AND GARLIC UNTIL SOFTENED. ADD THE MUSHROOMS AND GREEN PEPPERS AND SAUTE FOR 5 MINUTES.

ADD THE TEMPEH CUBES, TOMATOES (AND JUICES), HONEY, BASIL, AND OREGANO. BRING TO A BOIL, REDUCE HEAT, COVER PAN AND SIMMER FOR 10 MINUTES. UNCOVER AND SIMMER 10 MINUTES MORE. ADD SALT TO TASTE. SERVE OVER NOODLES OR SPAGHETTI.

ENJOY!

No. 7.

No. 8.

No. 9.

No. 10.

NIGERIAN SAUTÉ

SERVES 4

1 LARGE ONION, CHOPPED
2 CLOVES GARLIC, MINCED
2 TBSP. SALAD OIL
8 OZ. TEMPEH, GRAIN OR SOY
1 LARGE TOMATO, CHOPPED
2 CUPS VEGETABLE OR CHICKEN STOCK
1 TBSP. CATSUP
1/2 CUP CRUNCHY STYLE PEANUT BUTTER
1/8 TSP. CAYENNE PEPPER
1 HARD BOILED EGG, SLICED
1/2 CUP ROASTED PEANUTS
HOT COOKED RICE

SAUTÉ ONION AND GARLIC IN OIL UNTIL THE ONION SOFTENS. CUT THE TEMPEH INTO 1 INCH CUBES. ADD TEMPEH CUBES AND CHOPPED TOMATO TO THE ONIONS AND SAUTÉ 5 MINUTES MORE, UNTIL THE TOMATO SOFTENS. ADD THE STOCK AND BRING TO A BOIL. STIR IN THE CATSUP, PEANUT BUTTER AND CAYENNE. LOWER HEAT, COVER AND SIMMER FOR 20 MINUTES, STIRRING OCCASIONALLY. ADD THE SLICED EGG AND PEANUTS JUST BEFORE SERVING.

SERVE OVER RICE.

DELICIOUS!

FRICASSÉED TEMPEH

SERVES 3 TO 4

2 TBSP. SALAD OIL
1 SMALL ONION, CHOPPED
1 CLOVE GARLIC, MINCED
1 CARROT, SLICED THIN
1/2 CUP CELERY, CHOPPED
7 TO 8 OZ. PRE-SEASONED TEMPEH
1/4 LB. MUSHROOMS, SLICED
1 CUP VEGETABLE STOCK OR WATER
1/2 TSP. SALT
1 TSP. WORCESTERSHIRE SAUCE
1 TBSP. CORNSTARCH
1/2 CUP MILK

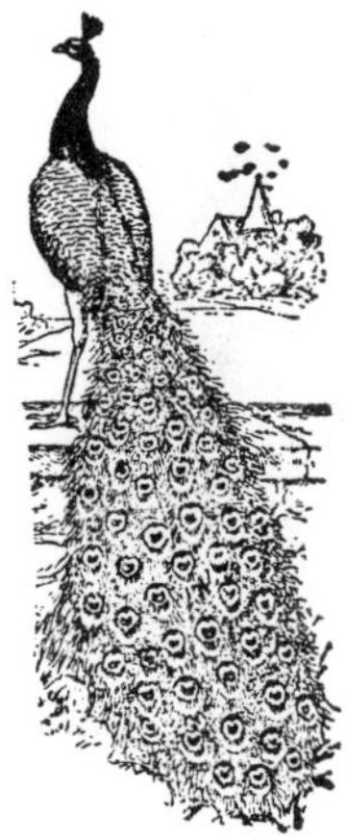

SAUTÉ THE ONION, GARLIC, CARROT, AND CELERY IN OIL UNTIL ONION SOFTENS. CUT THE TEMPEH INTO 1/2 INCH CUBES. ADD TEMPEH AND MUSHROOMS TO PAN AND SAUTÉ 3 MINUTES MORE. POUR IN THE STOCK OR WATER; COVER AND SIMMER 15 MINUTES. ADD SALT AND WORCESTERSHIRE SAUCE. STIR CORNSTARCH INTO THE MILK AND ADD TO TEMPEH AND VEGETABLES. COOK, STIRRING CONSTANTLY, UNTIL GRAVY THICKENS AND BOILS FOR 2 MINUTES. SERVE OVER RICE OR NOODLES WITH A DRY WHITE WINE.

PAPRIKA TEMPEH

SERVES 4

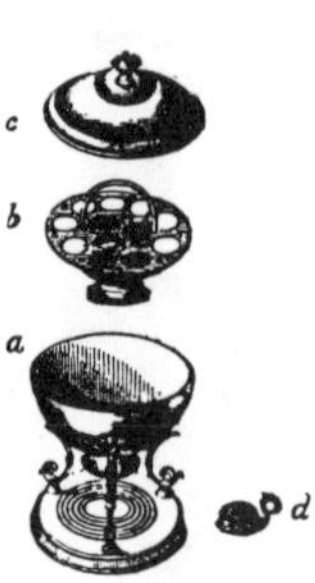

2 MILD ONIONS, THINLY SLICED
1/4 LB. MUSHROOMS, SLICED
2 TBSP. BUTTER OR MARGARINE
8 OZ. TEMPEH, GRAIN OR SOY
2 TBSP. SWEET PAPRIKA
1 CUP VEGETABLE OR CHICKEN STOCK
1 CUP SOUR CREAM OR YOGURT
8 OZ. COOKED EGG NOODLES

SAUTÉ ONIONS AND MUSHROOMS IN THE BUTTER OR MARGARINE IN A LARGE SKILLET UNTIL SOFT. CUT TEMPEH INTO 1/2 INCH CUBES. STIR PAPRIKA AND TEMPEH CUBES INTO THE SAUTÉED VEGETABLES. ADD STOCK, COVER AND SIMMER 20 MINUTES. REMOVE SKILLET FROM HEAT. PUSH TEMPEH MIXTURE TO ONE SIDE OF THE PAN AND SLOWLY ADD THE SOUR CREAM TO THE REMAINING STOCK, STIRRING CONSTANTLY. MIX GENTLY TO COAT THE TEMPEH MIXTURE WITH THE SOUR CREAM SAUCE. REHEAT OVER LOW HEAT UNTIL WARMED THROUGH. SERVE OVER HOT, BUTTERED NOODLES.

TEMPEH JOES

A BARBEQUE FAVORITE!

SERVES 4 TO 6

PRE-HEAT OVEN TO 350°

1 LB. TEMPEH, GRAIN OR SOY
2 TBSP. OIL
1 ONION, CHOPPED FINE
1 TO 2 CLOVES GARLIC, MINCED
16 OZ. TOMATO SAUCE. (2 CANS)
1 TBSP. VINEGAR
2 TBSP. HONEY OR BROWN SUGAR
1 TSP. WORCESTERSHIRE SAUCE
1/4 TSP. DRY MUSTARD

CUT TEMPEH INTO 1 INCH STRIPS AND PUT IN A SINGLE LAYER IN A BAKING DISH. SAUTÉ THE ONION AND GARLIC IN OIL UNTIL SOFT. ADD TOMATO SAUCE, VINEGAR, HONEY, WORCESTERSHIRE, AND MUSTARD. SIMMER FOR 10 MINUTES, STIRRING OCCAISIONALLY. POUR SAUCE OVER TEMPEH AND MARINATE, TURNING FREQUENTLY, FOR AT LEAST 20 MINUTES. REMOVE TEMPEH TO AN OILED BAKING SHEET. SPOON A GENEROUS AMOUNT OF MARINADE OVER TEMPEH AND BAKE AT 350° FOR 10 MINUTES. TURN TEMPEH OVER, SPOON MORE MARINADE ON TOP AND BAKE 10 MINUTES MORE. REPEAT THIS PROCEDURE ONCE MORE AND REMOVE FROM OVEN AND COOL SLIGHTLY BEFORE SERVING. SAVE REMAINING MARINADE TO SERVE WITH THE TEMPEH STRIPS.

THIS CAN BE MADE AHEAD AND REHEATED. SERVE IN BUNS FOR A BARBEQUE SANDWICH, OR TOP WITH RESERVED MARINADE AS A MAIN DISH.

NOTES

OVEN

H, was a Hopeful young Horse
Who was brought up on love without force
He had his own way
And ate tempeh with hay;
So he never was naughty of course!

GINGER BROIL

SERVES 4

1 LB. TEMPEH, GRAIN OR SOY
1 CUP PLAIN YOGURT
1 TSP. GINGER POWDER
1 TBSP. OIL
4 LARGE CLOVES GARLIC
1 TSP. CHILI POWDER
1/2 TSP. SALT, TO TASTE
1/2 TSP. PEPPER

CUT TEMPEH INTO 1 INCH PIECES. COMBINE REMAINING INGREDIENTS IN A BLENDER AND BLEND VERY SMOOTH. POUR OVER THE TEMPEH AND MARINATE IN THE REFRIGERATOR IN A COVERED CONTAINER.

BROIL, BASTING GENEROUSLY WITH THE MARINADE, UNTIL NICELY BROWNED. SERVE WITH RICE OR OVEN-FRIED POTATOES, AND A GREEN VEGETABLE.

OVEN FRIED POTATOES

SERVES 4

THERE IS NO TEMPEH IN THIS RECIPE, BUT IT IS SUCH A GREAT WAY TO FIX POTATOES, SO QUICK AND EASY, AND SO PERFECT WITH TEMPEH DISHES, THAT WE COULDN'T RESIST INCLUDING IT.

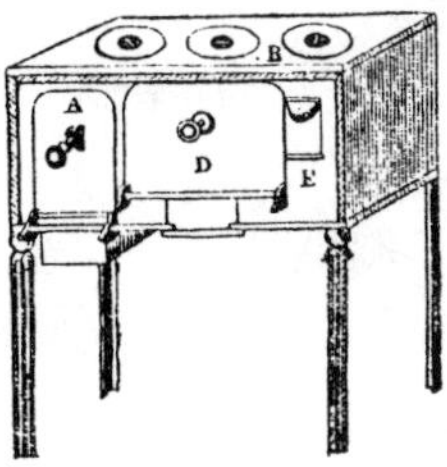

PREHEAT OVEN TO 425°

- 4 LARGE POTATOES
- OIL

SCRUB POTATOES WELL. CUT INTO "FRENCH FRY" TYPE PIECES OF ANY SIZE YOU LIKE, SKIN AND ALL. POUR A SMALL AMOUNT OF OIL IN A DISH AND COAT EACH PIECE OF POTATO WITH YOUR FINGERS. ARRANGE PIECES ON A BAKING SHEET SO THAT THEY DON'T OVERLAP AND BAKE IN 425° OVEN UNTIL GOLDEN BROWN, ABOUT 20 MINUTES. SERVE IMMEDIATELY!

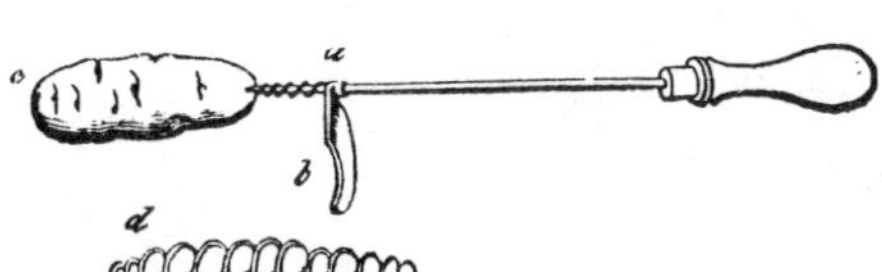

BROCCOLI BAKED TEMPEH

SERVES 4

PREHEAT OVEN TO 350°

2 TBSP. BUTTER OR MARGARINE
2 STALKS CELERY, CHOPPED
1 SMALL ONION, CHOPPED
8 OZ. TEMPEH, GRAIN OR SOY
10 OZ. PRE-COOKED BROCCOLI, CHOPPED
1 EGG
10 1/2 OZ. CREAM OF CELERY SOUP
1/2 CUP WHITE WINE OR CREAM
1 CUP GRATED CHEESE
1/2 CUP SLIVERED ALMONDS

MELT FAT IN A MEDIUM SKILLET. SAUTE CHOPPED CELERY AND ONION UNTIL SOFTENED. CUT TEMPEH INTO 1/2 INCH CUBES. ADD TO SKILLET AND SAUTÉ ABOUT 4 MINUTES, STIRRING OFTEN TO PREVENT STICKING. ADD COOKED BROCCOLI AND 1/4 CUP WATER. COVER AND SIMMER 5 MINUTES. TURN THE BROCCOLI-TEMPEH MIXTURE INTO A 2 QUART CASSEROLE.

MIX THE EGG, SOUP, WINE (OR CREAM) AND CHEESE. POUR OVER THE TEMPEH-BROCCOLI MIXTURE. SPRINKLE ALMONDS ON TOP. BAKE AT 350° FOR 25 MINUTES, OR UNTIL SAUCE IS BUBBLY AND ALMONDS LIGHTLY BROWNED. SERVE OVER NOODLES OR WITH BROWN RICE.

GARLIC TEMPEH WITH TURKEY

SERVES 6

<u>PREHEAT OVEN TO 325°</u>

2 TURKEY THIGHS, BONED, SKINNED (ABOUT 1 1/2 LBS.)
8 OZ. TEMPEH, GRAIN OR SOY (PLAIN OR PRE-SEASONED)
30 CLOVES GARLIC, UNPEELED
1 CUP CHOPPED CELERY
1/2 CUP DRY WHITE WINE
1/4 CUP MEDIUM DRY SHERRY
1/2 CUP WATER
1/4 CUP OLIVE OIL
1/2 TSP. DRIED TARRAGON
1/2 TSP. SALT (TO TASTE)
PEPPER TO TASTE
1 LEMON, JUICED

CUT TURKEY AND TEMPEH INTO BITE-SIZE PIECES. ARRANGE TURKEY, TEMPEH, GARLIC CLOVES, AND CELERY IN A TWO QUART CASSEROLE. SPRINKLE WINE, SHERRY, WATER, OLIVE OIL, TARRAGON, SALT AND PEPPER, AND LEMON JUICE OVER THE TOP. CUT UP LEMON RIND AND ADD TO THE CASSEROLE. COVER <u>VERY TIGHTLY</u> WITH FOIL AND ALSO WITH THE CASSEROLE LID. BAKE AT 325° FOR 1 1/2 HOURS. SERVE WITH BOILED POTATOES OR RICE. SQUEEZE THE GARLIC CLOVES OUT OF THEIR SKINS ONTO BREAD AND SPREAD LIKE BUTTER. DELICIOUS!

OR WITHOUT TURKEY — USE 3 8 OZ. PACKAGES OF TEMPEH IF YOU DON'T USE FOWL.

GRANNIE'S POT PIE

SERVES 8

TAKES AN HOUR TO PREPARE, AND WORTH EVERY MINUTE OF IT!

PREHEAT OVEN TO 400°

1 LARGE ONION
2 CARROTS, SLICED
2 CLOVES GARLIC, MINCED
2 STALKS CELERY, SLICED
2 TBSP. SALAD OIL
2 MEDIUM POTATOES
16 OZ. TEMPEH, SOY OR GRAIN
3 CUPS VEGETABLE OR CHICKEN STOCK
10 OZ. PKG. FROZEN PEAS, THAWED
1/4 CUP BUTTER OR MARGARINE
1/3 CUP FLOUR
SALT AND PEPPER TO TASTE
2 TSP. WORCESTERSHIRE SAUCE
1 1/2 CUPS BISCUIT MIX
1/2 CUP SOUR CREAM OR YOGURT
1 EGG
2 TSP. SESAME SEEDS

CUT ONION IN HALF LENGTHWISE AND SLICE. IN A LARGE SKILLET SAUTE ONION, CARROT, GARLIC, AND CELERY IN OIL UNTIL ONION SOFTENS. SCRUB BUT DON'T PEEL THE POTATOES AND CUT INTO 1/2 INCH PIECES. CUT TEMPEH INTO 1/2 INCH CUBES. ADD POTATOES AND TEMPEH TO SKILLET AND SAUTÉ FOR 3 MINUTES. POUR IN STOCK, COVER AND SIMMER 15 MINUTES. STIR IN PEAS AND REMOVE FROM HEAT.

POT PIE, CONT.

POUR TEMPEH AND VEGETABLES INTO A COLANDER WITH A LARGE BOWL UNDERNEATH TO CATCH THE STOCK. MEASURE STOCK AND ADD WATER TO MAKE 2 CUPS. MELT BUTTER OR MARGARINE IN SKILLET AND STIR IN FLOUR. COOK, STIRRING FOR 2 MINUTES. SLOWLY ADD THE STOCK. CONTINUE COOKING AND STIRRING UNTIL GRAVY. ADD WORCESTERSHIRE AND SALT AND PEPPER TO TASTE. POUR INTO A SHALLOW 2 QUART CASSEROLE.

CAN BE PREPARED AHEAD UP TO THIS POINT. COVER AND REFRIGERATE. 45 MINUTES BEFORE SERVING, REMOVE FROM REFRIGERATOR AND PREPARE THE BISCUIT TOPPING.

STIR TOGETHER BISCUIT MIX AND SOUR CREAM TO A FIRM STIFF DOUGH. TURN OUT ON A LIGHTLY FLOURED SURFACE AND KNEAD A FEW TIMES, THEN ROLL OUT 1 TO INCH LARGER THAN CASSEROLE. PLACE DOUGH OVER THE TEMPEH AND VEGETABLES, TURN EDGES UNDER EVEN WITH PAN RIM, AND FLUTE TO MAKE A PRETTY EDGE. CUT SEVERAL SLITS IN THE CENTER OF THE CRUST.

BEAT THE EGG WITH 1 TSP. WATER AND BRUSH OVER THE CRUST. SPRINKLE WITH SESAME SEEDS.

BAKE AT 400° FOR 30 MINUTES, UNTIL CRUST IS GOLDEN. COOL SLIGHTLY AND SERVE.
THIS DISH REHEATS WELL.

BANANA CURRY

SERVES 4

PREHEAT OVEN TO 350°

8 OZ. TEMPEH, GRAIN OR SOY
2 1/2 CUPS VEGETABLE OR CHICKEN STOCK
1/4 CUP BUTTER OR MARGARINE
1/4 CUP FLOUR
2 TSP. CURRY POWDER
SALT AND PEPPER TO TASTE
3 FIRM RIPE BANANAS
GRATED COCONUT (OPTIONAL)
HOT STEAMED RICE FOR 4

CUT TEMPEH INTO 1/2 INCH CUBES AND SIMMER IN THE STOCK FOR 10 MINUTES. REMOVE TEMPEH WITH A SLOTTED SPOON AND SET ASIDE. MEASURE STOCK AND ADD WATER TO MAKE 2 CUPS.

MELT FAT IN A SMALL SAUCEPAN. ADD FLOUR, CURRY POWDER, SALT, AND PEPPER AND BLEND WELL. GRADUALLY ADD THE STOCK AND COOK, STIRRING CONSTANTLY, UNTIL THE SAUCE IS SMOOTH AND THICKENED. PEEL BANANAS AND CUT INTO 1 INCH PIECES. PLACE THEM IN A 1 1/2 QUART CASSEROLE. POUR HALF THE CURRY SAUCE OVER THE BANANAS, COVER, AND BAKE AT 350° FOR 15 MINUTES. STIR THE TEMPEH AND REMAINING CURRY SAUCE INTO THE BANANAS, COVER AND BAKE 15 MINUTES MORE. SPRINKLE WITH COCONUT AND SPOON OVER RICE.

CHINESE BARBEQUE

USE INSTEAD OF BARBEQUED PORK IN YOUR FAVORITE CHINESE RECIPE.

8 OZ. TEMPEH, GRAIN OR SOY (CUT INTO 1 INCH STRIPS *)
3 TBSP. SOY SAUCE
3 TBSP. SHERRY
2 TBSP. HONEY
1 TBSP. WATER
1/4 TSP. CHINESE 5 SPICE POWDER
1 TBSP. SOY SAUCE
1 TBSP. OIL

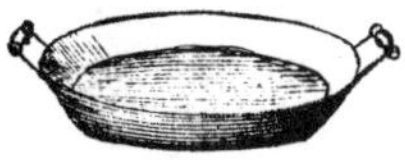

STIR TOGETHER SOY SAUCE, SHERRY, HONEY, WATER, AND CHINESE 5 SPICE IN A FLAT DISH. ADD TEMPEH STRIPS, TURNING, GENTLY, TO COAT WITH MARINADE. MARINATE 30 TO 40 MINUTES, TURNING OFTEN.

REMOVE TEMPEH STRIPS TO AN OILED BAKING SHEET. STIR TOGETHER 1 TBSP. SOY SAUCE, 1 TBSP. OIL, AND ANY REMAINING MARINADE. BRUSH TEMPEH WELL WITH THIS MIXTURE. BAKE AT 400° FOR 30° MINUTES. BASTE AND TURN TEMPEH STRIPS EVERY 5 MINUTES OR SO. TO USE, SLICE OR CUBE THE STRIPS AND ADD TO YOUR FAVORITE CHINESE DISH. GREAT IN FRIED RICE OR NOODLE DISHES!

* IF USING THICK TEMPEH (1 INCH OR MORE), CUT TEMPEH INTO 1/2 INCH STRIPS AND MARINATE CUT EDGES FIRST.

INDEX

END